TOUGH
QUESTIONS...
REAL ANSWERS
ABOUT
HOMOSEXUALITY

SMITH FREEMAN
Publishing

Tough Questions...Real Answers About Homosexuality

Bible verses were taken from the following translations:

ISBN 978-0-9986529-4-8

Contents

A Message to Readers

What does God say about homosexuality? Or same-sex unions? Or gay marriage? The answer is straightforward: God's Word teaches us that homosexuality is wrong because it's not part of His plan for humanity. But here in twenty-first-century America, cultural norms have changed. Now, large segments of society endorse the gay lifestyle and, in many cases, promote it. So what's a Christian to do? The answer, simply put, is to stand firm on the Biblical truths and encourage others to do the same.

Perhaps you have a family member who has recently announced that he or she is gay. Or perhaps you are struggling with homosexual urges of your own. In either case, this book is intended to help by giving you God's perspective on the topic.

As Christians, we are commanded to love all our neighbors, which includes homosexuals. So when dealing with gay family members or friends, we must leave no room in our hearts for hatred or animosity. But what we can do is this: we can build our own lives on the promises and teachings found in God's Word. We can pray for our loved ones, we can talk constructively with them, and we can offer assistance if they genuinely want to seek help. Then, when we've done our best, we must leave the rest up to God.

Perhaps you never dreamed that one day you'd be reading a book about homosexuality. If so, you may be upset, confused, or even confounded by the topic. If that is the case, please remember that no challenge is too big God...not even yours. Nothing is impossible for Him, so don't abandon hope. In His own time and in His own way, the Lord blesses those who trust Him. Please count yourself among that number.

Six Things to Remember about Homosexuality

The Bible clearly states that homosexuality is a sin. To see for yourself, check out Leviticus 18:22, 1 Timothy 1:9–11, and 1 Corinthians 6:9–10.

Although many segments of modern culture endorse homosexuality and same-sex marriage, Christians should trust God's Word. Societal norms change; God's Word doesn't.

While homosexuality is a sin, it's not an unforgivable sin. We're all sinners, and God's mercy is available to all of us whenever we seek it.

Whenever we continue to engage in behaviors that are displeasing to God, we inevitably do ourselves harm. And so it is with homosexual urges: obedience pays; disobedience doesn't.

If you have same-sex feelings that are making you uncomfortable, counseling is available. Your pastoral counselor is a great place to start.

God's Word commands us to show love and respect to all people, including homosexuals. No exceptions.

1

The Question

Everywhere I turn, it seems like people are praising homosexuality and, in many cases, glamorizing it. What does the Bible say?

The Answer

The Bible clearly states that homosexual relations are sinful. To see for yourself, check out Leviticus 18:22, 1 Timothy 1:9–11, and 1 Corinthians 6:9–10. It's right there in black and white.

Run from sexual immorality!... The person who is sexually immoral sins against his own body. Don't you know that your body is a sanctuary of the Holy Spirit who is in you, whom you have from God? You are not your own, for you were bought at a price. Therefore glorify God in your body.

1 CORINTHIANS 6:18–20 HCSB

What the Bible Says about Homosexuality

*You are not to sleep with a man
as with a woman; it is detestable.*
LEVITICUS 18:22 HCSB

Modern society praises, endorses, and even glorifies homosexuality. But the Bible does not. God's Word makes it clear that sexual relations are acceptable only inside marriage, and that marriage is an institution created for a man and a woman.

For Christians who choose to use the Bible as their guidebook for life, there's no room for interpretation: Homosexuality is a sin, and those who continue to engage in homosexuality are, according to God's Word, continuing to engage in sin. Period. But the media teaches—and preaches—otherwise.

Modern media bombards us with messages that are contrary to our spiritual health. And many segments of society now approve and support the gay lifestyle. So as Christians we must choose between society's value system and God's value system. The choice should be obvious.

More from God's Word

Be sober, be vigilant; because your adversary
the devil walks about like a roaring lion,
seeking whom he may devour.
1 PETER 5:8 NKJV

Put on the full armor of God so that you
can stand against the tactics of the Devil.
EPHESIANS 6:11 HCSB

Therefore submit to God. Resist the devil and he will
flee from you. Draw near to God and He will draw
near to you. Cleanse your hands, you sinners;
and purify your hearts, you double-minded.
JAMES 4:7–8 NKJV

Don't fear those who kill the body but are not able
to kill the soul; rather, fear Him who is able
to destroy both soul and body in hell.
MATTHEW 10:28 HCSB

Dear friend, do not imitate what is evil, but what
is good. The one who does good is of God;
the one who does evil has not seen God.
3 JOHN 1:11 HCSB

More Thoughts about God's Truth

A lie doesn't become a truth and wrong doesn't become right and evil doesn't become good just because it's popular. Truth is truth.

RICK WARREN

Those who walk in truth walk in liberty.

BETH MOORE

We learn His truth by obeying it.

OSWALD CHAMBERS

Truth will triumph. The Father of truth will win, and the followers of truth will be saved.

MAX LUCADO

Spiritual truth is discernable only to a pure heart, not to a keen intellect. It is not a question of intellect, but of purity of heart.

OSWALD CHAMBERS

2

The Question

The popular media glamorizes homosexuality and the gay lifestyle. Should I believe the media?

The Answer

When the media glamorizes homosexuality, it is spreading a message that is contrary to God's Word. The media's messages are often misleading but God's Word will never lead you astray. Trust God.

*We need more love for the Word
and less love for the world.*

R. G. LEE

General Confusion, Gender Confusion

If a man practices homosexuality,
having sex with another man as with a woman,
both men have committed a detestable act.
LEVITICUS 20:13 NLT

The twenty-first-century world in which we live is a noisy, confusing place. Part of the confusion stems from the fact that every day, twenty-four hours a day, the media manages to generate a host of messages that are simply untrue. One of those messages concerns homosexuality. The "popular" media would have us believe that homosexual relations are acceptable, normal, and proper. But God's Word clearly says otherwise. The Bible defines homosexuality as sin—not an unforgiveable sin but a sin nonetheless. And those of us who intend to use the Bible as our guide for life must take God at His word.

We live in this world, but we should not worship it. Yet we are bombarded by deceptive messages that tempt us to place the world's values above God's values. Such are the dangers and temptations of being too enamored with the world's values.

If we are wise and obedient, we won't worship the world. We will worship God and honor His commandments about sexuality and every other aspect of our lives.

More from God's Word

And do not be conformed to this world,
but be transformed by the renewing of your mind,
that you may prove what is that good
and acceptable and perfect will of God.

ROMANS 12:2 NKJV

For our citizenship is in heaven, from which also
we eagerly wait for a Savior, the Lord Jesus Christ.

PHILIPPIANS 3:20 NASB

No one can serve two masters. For you will hate
one and love the other; you will be devoted to one
and despise the other. You cannot serve God
and be enslaved to money.

LUKE 16:13 NLT

Don't you know that friendship with the world
is hostility toward God? So whoever wants
to be the world's friend becomes God's enemy.

JAMES 4:4 HCSB

Set your mind on the things above,
not on the things that are on earth.

COLOSSIANS 3:2 NASB

More Thoughts about Worldliness

The voices of the world are a cacophony of chaos,
pulling you this way and that. Don't listen
to those voices.

SARAH YOUNG

Loving the world destroys our relationship with God,
it denies our faith in God, and it discounts
our future with God.

DAVID JEREMIAH

Our fight is not against any physical enemy;
it is against organizations and powers that are
spiritual. We must struggle against sin all our lives,
but we are assured we will win.

CORRIE TEN BOOM

We live in a hostile world that constantly
seeks to pull us away from God.

BILLY GRAHAM

If you are a Christian, you are not a citizen of this
world trying to get to heaven; you are a citizen
of heaven making your way through this world.

VANCE HAVNER

3

The Question

Many of my friends are trying to convince me that homosexuality is a perfectly acceptable lifestyle. Are they right?

The Answer

Your friends are wrong. God's Word clearly states that homosexuality is a sin. The Bible is unambiguous in its condemnation of homosexuality. You should trust God, not your peers.

A man with God is always in the majority.

JOHN KNOX

Pressure from Society, Pressure from Peers

Do not be mismatched with unbelievers.
For what partnership is there between
righteousness and lawlessness?
Or what fellowship does light have with darkness?
2 CORINTHIANS 6:14 HCSB

Your world is filled with pressures: some good, some not so good, and some downright tragic. The pressures you feel to honor your Father in heaven and obey His holy Word are good pressures. They make you a better person and a better Christian. But the pressures you feel to follow the crowd and thus distance yourself from God are bad pressures. They're dangerous to your spiritual, emotional, and physical health.

It makes no difference what your friends say about homosexuality—or any other topic, for that matter. It's what God says that matters.

So whom will you try to please today: your peers or your Father in heaven? The answer should be obvious. If you invest time and energy in trying to please people, you'll find it an unending, unfulfilling task. But if you strive to please God first and always, you'll be blessed. So if there's ever a choice between going along with the crowd or going along with God, choose God. It's the safe way—and the best way—to live.

More from God's Word

Dear friend, do not imitate what is evil, but what is good. The one who does good is of God; the one who does evil has not seen God.
3 JOHN 1:11 HCSB

But Peter and the apostles replied, "We must obey God rather than men."
ACTS 5:29 HCSB

Do you think I am trying to make people accept me? No, God is the One I am trying to please. Am I trying to please people? If I still wanted to please people, I would not be a servant of Christ.
GALATIANS 1:10 NCV

My son, if sinners entice you, don't be persuaded.
PROVERBS 1:10 HCSB

Do not be deceived: "Bad company corrupts good morals."
1 CORINTHIANS 15:33 HCSB

More Thoughts about Peer Pressure and Society's Pressure

Many Christians give in to various temptations through peer pressure. They find themselves surrendering to worldly passions, justifying pleasures the world offers.

BILLY GRAHAM

Tell me with whom thou art found, and I will tell thee who thou art.

JOHANN WOLFGANG VON GOETHE

For better or worse, you will eventually become more and more like the people you associate with. So why not associate with people who make you better, not worse?

MARIE T. FREEMAN

Loving God—really loving Him—means living out His commands no matter what the cost.

CHARLES COLSON

Happiness is obedience and obedience is happiness.

C. H. SPURGEON

4

The Question

It seems like society wants me to endorse
homosexuality and gay marriage.
What should I do?

The Answer

As a Christian, your obligation is to honor God
and obey Him, popular culture notwithstanding.
God wants you to guard your heart
by giving it to Him.

*We should say nothing that we would not wish
to say in His presence. We should do nothing
that we would not do in His presence.*

BILLY GRAHAM

Guard Your Heart

Guard your heart above all else,
for it is the source of life.
PROVERBS 4:23 HCSB

God's Word is clear: we are to guard our hearts "above all else." Yet here in the twenty-first century, false messages and false promises are woven into everyday life. Many famous people endorse behaviors that are contrary to God's will and His plan for mankind. We are told that homosexuality is perfectly normal and perfectly harmless. But the Bible offers a different interpretation, and as believers, we must remain vigilant. Not only must we resist Satan when he confronts us, but we must also avoid the people and the places where Satan can most easily engage us.

Do you seek God's peace and His blessings? Then guard your heart above all else. When you're faced with a difficult choice or a powerful temptation, seek God's counsel and trust the counsel He gives. When you're uncertain of your next step, calm down, take a deep breath, and follow in the footsteps of God's only begotten Son. Invite God into your heart and live according to His commandments. When you do, you will be blessed today and tomorrow and forever.

More from God's Word

Blessed are the pure in heart, for they will see God.
MATTHEW 5:8 NIV

*Flee from youthful passions, and pursue
righteousness, faith, love, and peace, along
with those who call on the Lord from a pure heart.*
2 TIMOTHY 2:22 HCSB

*The peace of God, which surpasses
all understanding, will guard your hearts
and minds through Christ Jesus.*
PHILIPPIANS 4:7 NKJV

*The one who keeps God's commands lives in him,
and he in them. And this is how we know that he
lives in us: We know it by the Spirit he gave us.*
1 JOHN 3:24 NIV

*Finally, brothers and sisters, whatever is true,
whatever is noble, whatever is right,
whatever is pure, whatever is lovely,
whatever is admirable—if anything is excellent
or praiseworthy—think about such things.*
PHILIPPIANS 4:8 NIV

More Thoughts about Guarding Your Heart

Our battles are first won or lost in the secret places of our will in God's presence, never in full view of the world.

OSWALD CHAMBERS

No matter how many pleasures Satan offers you, his ultimate intention is to ruin you. Your destruction is his highest priority.

ERWIN LUTZER

The insight that relates to God comes from purity of heart, not from clearness of intellect.

OSWALD CHAMBERS

The whole history of the world is discovered to be but a contest between the wisdom of God and the cunning of Satan and fallen men. The outcome of the contest is not in doubt.

A. W. TOZER

It is only by obedience that we understand the teaching of God.

OSWALD CHAMBERS

5

The Question

Some of my favorite entertainers are gay.
Does that mean that homosexuality is okay?

The Answer

It makes no difference what your friends say
or what famous people do. You must honor God
by understanding His teachings and obeying
His commandments.

*Homosexual behavior has been exploited,
and reveled in, and celebrated in art, for millennia.
What's new is normalization and institutionalization.
This is the new calamity.*

JOHN PIPER

Rewriting the Rules

So God abandoned them to do whatever shameful things their hearts desired. As a result, they did vile and degrading things with each other's bodies. They traded the truth about God for a lie. So they worshiped and served the things God created instead of the Creator himself, who is worthy of eternal praise! Amen. That is why God abandoned them to their shameful desires. Even the women turned against the natural way to have sex and instead indulged in sex with each other. And the men, instead of having normal sexual relations with women, burned with lust for each other. Men did shameful things with other men, and as a result of this sin, they suffered within themselves the penalty they deserved.

ROMANS 1:24–27 NLT

Sometimes it's hard being a faithful Christian, especially when the world keeps pumping out messages that are contrary to our faith.

The media is working around the clock to attempt to rearrange our priorities and upend our value system. The media says, among other things, that homosexuality is simply an "alternative lifestyle," a perfectly acceptable choice for those who find themselves attracted to members of the same sex. These messages are contrary to God's Word and, therefore, dangerous to our spiritual, moral, and emotional health.

So do yourself a favor: Ignore the media messages and pay careful attention, instead, to God's messages. Stand up for Him and be counted, not just in church where it's relatively easy to be a Christian, but also outside the church, where it's significantly harder. You owe it the Lord. And you owe it to yourself.

More from God's Word

*The righteousness of the blameless clears his path,
but the wicked person will fall
because of his wickedness.*

PROVERBS 11:5 HCSB

*So I strive always to keep my conscience clear
before God and man.*

ACTS 24:16 NIV

*Let us come near to God with a sincere heart
and a sure faith, because we have been made
free from a guilty conscience, and our bodies
have been washed with pure water.*

HEBREWS 10:22 NCV

*If then you were raised with Christ, seek those things
which are above, where Christ is, sitting at the right
hand of God. Set your mind on things above,
not on things on the earth.*

COLOSSIANS 3:1–2 NKJV

*Do not conform to the pattern of this world,
but be transformed by the renewing of your mind.
Then you will be able to test and approve what
God's will is—his good, pleasing and perfect will.*

ROMANS 12:2 NIV

More Thoughts about Modern Media and Worldly Values

Our fight is not against any physical enemy; it is against organizations and powers that are spiritual. We must struggle against sin all our lives, but we are assured we will win.

CORRIE TEN BOOM

The media relentlessly proclaim bad news: for breakfast, lunch, and dinner. A steady diet of their fare will sicken you. Instead of focusing on fickle, ever-changing news broadcasts, tune in to the living Word.

SARAH YOUNG

Popularity is far more dangerous for the Christian than persecution.

BILLY GRAHAM

Reading news without reading the Bible will inevitably lead to an unbalanced life, an anxious spirit, a worried and depressed soul.

BILL BRIGHT

There's not a thing wrong with television that not watching it won't cure.

FRANKLIN P. JONES

6

The Question

I've had homosexual urges.
What should I do about them?

The Answer

Since God's Word brands homosexuality a sin,
you must resist those urges using every tool at your
disposal, including prayer, worship, Bible study,
and pastoral counseling.

*A person who wrestles with homosexual
temptations and desires has the same choice:
to sin with it or to be chaste, seek
to overcome, and move into something
more God-appointed.*

JOHN PIPER

The Enemy Never Rests

Your adversary, the devil, prowls around like
a roaring lion, seeking someone to devour.
1 PETER 5:8 NASB

It's not a sin to be tempted; it's a sin to give into the temptation. And so it is with homosexuality. It's not a sin to be attracted to a member of the same sex; it's a sin to act upon that temptation.

The devil, it seems, is causing pain and heartache in more places and in more ways than ever before. We, as Christians, must remain vigilant. Not only must we resist Satan when he confronts us, but we must also avoid those places where Satan can most easily tempt us. And if we are to avoid the unending temptations of this world, we must earnestly wrap ourselves in the protection of God's holy Word.

When it comes to fighting temptation, you are never alone. God is always with you. And if you do your part, He will do His part. But what, precisely, is your part? A good starting point is simply learning how to recognize the subtle temptations that surround you. The images of immorality are ubiquitous, and they're intended to hijack your mind, your heart, your life, and your soul. Don't let them do it.

The road to ruin is wide, long, and deadly. Avoid it, and help others do the same. When you do, God will smile—and the devil won't.

More from God's Word

No temptation has overtaken you but such
as is common to man; and God is faithful,
who will not allow you to be tempted beyond
what you are able, but with the temptation
will provide the way of escape.
1 CORINTHIANS 10:13 NASB

Do not be misled: "Bad company
corrupts good character."
1 CORINTHIANS 15:33 NIV

Put on the whole armor of God, that you may
be able to stand against the wiles of the devil.
EPHESIANS 6:11 NKJV

But encourage each other daily, while it is still
called today, so that none of you is hardened
by sin's deception.
HEBREWS 3:13 HCSB

Let us lay aside every weight, and the sin which
so easily ensnares us, and let us run with endurance
the race that is set before us.
HEBREWS 12:1 NKJV

More Thoughts
about Temptation

*I do not believe that attraction is a sin,
but I do believe that some actions are sin.*

RICK WARREN

*We must confront sin with the truth of scripture
and the love of the Lord Jesus Christ.*

CHARLES STANLEY

*Do today's duty; fight today's temptation;
do not weaken and distract yourself by looking
forward to things you cannot see, and could
not understand if you saw them.*

CHARLES KINGSLEY

*If your mind is filled with the Word of God,
then it can't be filled with impure thoughts.*

DAVID JEREMIAH

*It is impossible to please God doing things
motivated by and produced by the flesh.*

BILL BRIGHT

7

The Question

The Bible says that homosexuality is a sin. So what does that mean for people who are gay?

The Answer

Homosexuality is a sin, but it's not an unforgivable sin. We all are sinners, and God is merciful. His grace and His forgiveness are available to all of us. All we need to do is ask.

We affirm God's plan for marriage and sexual intimacy—one man and one woman, for life. Homosexuality is not a "valid alternative lifestyle." The Bible condemns it as sin. It is not, however, unforgivable sin. The same redemption available to all sinners is available to homosexuals. They, too, may become new creations in Christ.
SOUTHERN BAPTIST CONVENTION

The Struggle against Sin

Test all things; hold fast what is good.
Abstain from every form of evil.
1 Thessalonians 5:21–22 NKJV

What is sin? For Christians, the answer to this question can be found between the covers of the Holy Bible. If the Bible defines an activity as sin, it's a sin. Period.

God's Word clearly describes homosexuality as sin. References are found in both the Old and New Testaments, and these passages are unambiguous. Homosexuality, like many other transgressions, is contrary to God's plan for mankind. He has warned us against it, and if we're wise, we'll take His warnings seriously.

Homosexuality is not an unforgivable sin. Thankfully, God's mercy is available to all. When we ask the Lord to forgive us, He wraps us in His mercy and love. But if we continue to live outside His will for our lives, He doesn't protect us from the consequences of our mistakes.

As creatures of free will, we may disobey God whenever we choose, but to do so is shortsighted and dangerous. Disobedience invites disaster. We cannot sin against God without consequence. We cannot live outside His will without harming ourselves and our loved ones. We cannot distance ourselves from God without hardening our hearts.

Sins of all shapes and sizes have the power to do us great harm. And so it is with homosexuality. It's a behavior that God doesn't condone, and neither should we.

More from God's Word

*Let us lay aside every weight and the sin that so
easily ensnares us, Let us run with endurance the
race that lies before us, keeping our eyes on Jesus,
the source and perfecter of our faith.*

HEBREWS 12:1–2 HCSB

*Take heed, brethren, lest there be in any of you
an evil heart of unbelief, in departing from the living
God. But exhort one another daily, while it is called
To day; lest any of you be hardened through
the deceitfulness of sin.*

HEBREWS 3:12–13 KJV

*Don't be deceived: God is not mocked.
For whatever a man sows he will also reap,
because the one who sows to his flesh will reap
corruption from the flesh, but the one who sows
to the Spirit will reap eternal life from the Spirit.*

GALATIANS 6:7–8 HCSB

*Therefore submit to God. Resist the devil and he will
flee from you. Draw near to God and He will draw
near to you. Cleanse your hands, you sinners;
and purify your hearts, you double-minded.*

JAMES 4:7–8 NKJV

*Little children, let no one deceive you! The one who
does what is right is righteous, just as He is righteous.
The one who commits sin is of the Devil,
for the Devil has sinned from the beginning.*

1 JOHN 3:7–8 HCSB

More Thoughts
about God's Forgiveness

We cannot out-sin God's ability to forgive us.

BETH MOORE

*God's mercy is boundless, free,
and, through Jesus Christ our Lord,
available to us in our present situation.*

A. W. TOZER

*Forgiveness is an opportunity that God extended to
us on the cross. When we accept His forgiveness and
are willing to forgive ourselves, then we find relief.*

BILLY GRAHAM

*God's forgiveness is always free. But that doesn't
mean that confession is always easy. Sometimes
it is hard. Incredibly hard. It is painful to admit
our sins and entrust ourselves to God's care.*

ERWIN LUTZER

*The love of God overwhelms me with acceptance,
forgiveness, compassion, and joy in believing.*

BILL BRIGHT

8

The Question

Sometimes it's hard to be an obedient Christian, especially when so many people are endorsing things that seem contrary to God's Word. What does the Bible say about obedience?

The Answer

God's Word is clear: We must obey Him or face the consequences. The Lord rewards obedience and punishes disobedience. So it's not enough to understand His rules; you must also live by them.

Let us never suppose that obedience is impossible or that holiness is meant only for a select few. Our Shepherd leads us in paths of righteousness— not for our name's sake but for His.

ELISABETH ELLIOT

Trust and Obey

Trust in the LORD with all your heart, and lean not on your own understanding; in all your ways acknowledge Him, and He shall direct your paths.

PROVERBS 3:5–6 NKJV

God's instructions to mankind are contained in a book like no other: the Holy Bible. When we obey God's commandments and listen carefully to the conscience He has placed in our hearts, we are secure. But if we disobey our Creator, if we choose to ignore the teachings and the warnings of His Word, we do so at great peril.

God's Word clearly instructs us that homosexuality is contrary to His plan for mankind. Yet powerful forces are at work, forces that embrace the gay lifestyle and endorse same-sex marriage. As Christians, we owe our allegiance to our Father in heaven, not to popular culture or to worldly institutions.

Susanna Wesley said, "There are two things to do about the gospel: believe it and behave it." Her words serve as a powerful reminder that, as Christians, we are called to take God's warnings seriously and live in accordance with His teachings.

God gave us His commandments for a reason: so that we might obey them and be blessed. Yet we live in a world that presents us with countless temptations to stray far from His path. It is our responsibility to resist those temptations with vigor. Obedience isn't just the *best* way to experience the full measure of God's blessings; it's the only way.

More from God's Word

Those who trust in the LORD are like Mount Zion.
It cannot be shaken; it remains forever.
PSALM 125:1 HCSB

Jesus said, "Don't let your hearts be troubled.
Trust in God, and trust in me."
JOHN 14:1 NCV

Now by this we know that we know Him,
if we keep His commandments.
1 JOHN 2:3 NKJV

Praise the LORD! Happy are those who respect
the LORD, who want what he commands.
PSALM 112:1 NCV

Teach me, O LORD, the way of Your statutes,
and I shall observe it to the end.
PSALM 119:33 NASB

More Thoughts about Obedience

*Let the church be a house of compassion.
But let her also be a house of conviction.
The Holy Scripture was the first code to call man
and women to rein in their sexual desires and
express them under the covenant of male-female
marriage. Homosexual union then is not a step
forward, but a step backward. A step back into
the society from which God delivered us.*

MAX LUCADO

Obedience is the key to every door.

GEORGE MACDONALD

*Obedience is a foundational stepping-stone
on the path of God's will.*

ELIZABETH GEORGE

*Never be afraid to trust an unknown future
to a known God.*

CORRIE TEN BOOM

*Never imagine that you can be a loser
by trusting in God.*

C. H. SPURGEON

9

The Question

God's Word warns that homosexuality is a sin. But the world says otherwise. Who's right?

The Answer

In all matters, you must trust God's holy Word. The Bible is God's truth expressed to mankind. You must read it, believe it, and live it.

We will encourage that persons with same-sex attraction understand the reality of God's Word and seek to avail themselves of the hope that is found in the gospel.

FRANK PAGE

Trust God's Word

*All scripture is given by inspiration of God,
and is profitable for doctrine, for reproof,
for correction, for instruction in righteousness.*
2 TIMOTHY 3:16 KJV

If you're dealing with feelings that are contrary to God's teachings, talk to Him and study His Word. God's promises never fail, and His truth endures forever. And if you'd like to experience His peace, Bible study can help provide it.

Warren Wiersbe observed, "When the child of God looks into the Word of God, he sees the Son of God. And he is transformed by the Spirit of God to share in the glory of God." The Holy Word is, indeed, a life-changing, spirit-lifting, one-of-a-kind treasure. And it's up to you—and only you—to use it that way.

Jonathan Edwards advised, "Be assiduous in reading the Holy Scriptures. This is the fountain whence all knowledge in divinity must be derived. Therefore let not this treasure lie by you neglected." God's Holy Word is, indeed, a priceless, one-of-a-kind treasure. Handle it with care, but more importantly, handle it every day. When you do, the Lord will speak to you in those quiet moments and give you the direction you need to fulfill His will.

More from God's Word

The counsel of the LORD stands forever, the plans
of His heart from generation to generation.
PSALM 33:11 NASB

But whoever looks intently into the perfect law that
gives freedom, and continues in it—
not forgetting what they have heard, but doing it—
they will be blessed in what they do.
JAMES 1:25 NIV

But grow in the grace and knowledge of our Lord
and Savior Jesus Christ. To Him be the glory both
now and to the day of eternity.
2 PETER 3:18 HCSB

But the word of the Lord endures forever. And this
is the word that was preached as the gospel to you.
1 PETER 1:25 HCSB

You will be a good servant of Christ Jesus,
nourished by the words of the faith and the good
teaching that you have followed.
1 TIMOTHY 4:6 HCSB

More Thoughts about Bible Study

*Do you want your faith to grow? Then let the Bible
began to saturate your mind and soul.*

BILLY GRAHAM

*I believe the reason so many are failing today
is that they have not disciplined themselves
to read God's Word consistently, day in and day
out, and to apply it to every situation in life.*

KAY ARTHUR

*Reading the Bible has a purifying effect upon your
life. Let nothing take the place of this daily exercise.*

BILLY GRAHAM

*Read the scripture, not only as history,
but as a love letter sent to you from God.*

THOMAS WATSON

*Gather the riches of God's promises. Nobody can
take away from you those texts from the Bible
which you have learned by heart.*

CORRIE TEN BOOM

10

The Question

I know people who are gay.
How am I supposed to treat them?

The Answer

As Christians, we are commanded to love others.
God wants us to cleanse our hearts of bitterness
and hatred. We must behave accordingly.

—~~—

*Yes, homosexual activity angers God. But who
among us has not angered God? It wasn't
homosexuality that caused Jesus to cleanse
the Temple. It was self-righteousness and greed:
two sins that dog all of us. Let there be no gay
bashing among God's people.*

MAX LUCADO

And the Greatest of These Is Love

But now faith, hope, love, abide these three;
but the greatest of these is love.

1 CORINTHIANS 13:13 NASB

As Christians, we are commanded to love our neighbors as ourselves, and the term "our neighbors" includes homosexuals. Because we seek to follow Christ, we must treat all people, both gay and straight, in the way we would wish to be treated if we were in their shoes. No exceptions.

Love, like everything else in this world, begins and ends with God, but the middle part belongs to us. The Creator gives each of us the opportunity to be kind, courteous, and loving. He gives each of us the chance to obey the Golden Rule or to make up our own rules as we go. If we obey God's instructions, we're secure, but if we do otherwise, we suffer.

Christ's words are clear: "This is My command: Love one another as I have loved you" (John 15:12 HCSB). We are clearly instructed to love all people, but because we are imperfect, we often fall short. When we become embittered against our neighbors—when we mock, scorn, or deride them—we disobey and dishonor the One who gave His life for us. Christ showed His love for us on the cross, and, as Christians, we are called upon to return Christ's love by sharing it. No exceptions.

More from God's Word

A new commandment I give unto you,
That ye love one another; as I have loved you,
that ye also love one another.

John 13:34 KJV

Love is patient, love is kind. Love does not envy,
is not boastful, is not conceited.

1 Corinthians 13:4 HCSB

Beloved, if God so loved us,
we ought also to love one another.

1 John 4:11 KJV

Above all, love each other deeply,
because love covers over a multitude of sins.

1 Peter 4:8 NIV

And we have known and believed the love
that God has for us. God is love, and he who
abides in love abides in God, and God in him.

1 John 4:16 NKJV

More Thoughts about Love

The love life of the Christian is a crucial battleground. There, if nowhere else, it will be determined who is Lord: the world, the self, and the devil—or the Lord Christ.

ELISABETH ELLIOT

The vast ocean of Love cannot be measured or explained, but it can be experienced.

SARAH YOUNG

Love always means sacrifice.

ELISABETH ELLIOT

Line by line, moment by moment, special times are etched into our memories in the permanent ink of everlasting love in our relationships.

GLORIA GAITHER

Love does not dominate; it cultivates.

JOHANN WOLFGANG VON GOETHE

11

The Question

What about gay marriage?
Isn't it supposed to be the law of the land?

The Answer

The Bible is clear—God's definition of marriage
is between a man and a woman.

—⟋⟍⟍—

*God created marriage. No government
subcommittee envisioned it. No social organization
developed it. Marriage was conceived
and born in the mind of God.*

MAX LUCADO

Marriage according to God

*Therefore a man shall leave his father
and mother and be joined to his wife,
and they shall become one flesh.*

Genesis 2:24 NKJV

The Bible defines marriage as the union between a man and a woman. Since the dawn of humanity, that definition was taken for granted in most cultures: one man and one woman, joined together in matrimony for life. No more. Today, societal forces and governmental institutions have hastily endorsed same-sex marriage without regard to biblical truths or long-standing cultural norms.

So what are we, as Christians, to make of the rush to sanction, to ratify, and to applaud gay marriage? If we trust God's Word, we must stand in opposition to same-sex unions. Simply put, gay marriage is an institution that God does not condone, and neither should we.

More from God's Word

A virtuous woman is a crown to her husband.
PROVERBS 12:4 KJV

Marriage must be respected by all, and the marriage bed kept undefiled, because God will judge immoral people and adulterers.
HEBREWS 13:4 HCSB

But because sexual sin is a danger, each man should have his own wife, and each woman should have her own husband.
1 CORINTHIANS 7:2 NCV

But I want you to understand this: The head of every man is Christ, the head of a woman is the man, and the head of Christ is God.
1 CORINTHIANS 11:3 HCSB

*Who can find a virtuous wife?
For her worth is far above rubies.*
PROVERBS 31:10 NKJV

More Thoughts about Marriage

While we affirm our love for all people, including those struggling with same-sex attraction, we cannot and will not affirm any behavior that deviates from God's design for marriage.

RONNIE FLOYD

To redefine marriage would destroy the picture that God intends for marriage to portray, and we cannot cave on this issue.

RICK WARREN

The Bible is God's final authority about marriage, and on this Book we stand.

RONNIE FLOYD

God categorically opposes gay marriage. It violates his plan for man-woman permanence. It frustrates and denies complementariness in nurturing. The church must stand with her Maker on this issue. Too much is at stake.

MAX LUCADO

Same-sex marriage undermines God's plan for the family. Weakened families impact society.

MAX LUCADO

12

The Question

I have an adult family member who has
announced that he (or she) is gay.
What should I do?

The Answer

You must find ways to love your family member
without endorsing any behavior that is contrary
to God's will or God's Word. Pray for your family
member, and pray for healing. With God,
all things are possible.

*Ex-gays worshipped in the early church. Ex-gays
worship in this church. For those of you who struggle
with this issue, be assured, you are welcome here.
Should you desire help, we have people
who stand ready to offer it.*

MAX LUCADO

Homosexuality in the Family

Choose for yourselves this day whom you will serve.... But as for me and my house, we will serve the LORD.

JOSHUA 24:15 NKJV

What should you do if a close family member announces that he or she is gay? It's a difficult question that many Christians must face. Below are several ideas from Focus on the Family, recommending how Christian parents should react to the announcement from an adult son, who is still living at home (2016).

Don't assume responsibility for decisions your son has made as an autonomous adult. He's old enough to be his own person, and a burden of false guilt will only hinder you from showing him God's love in the most effective way.

Treat him as you would any other adult who is old enough to choose his own path in life.

If he wishes to remain in your home, he should know the house rules, respect your beliefs and values, and agree to abide by the standards you've established in order to ensure the safety, security, and well-being of every member of the family.

If your son decides that he cannot abide by your guidelines, invite him to begin the process of moving out of the house and pursuing his newfound lifestyle in an independent setting.

If he persists in arguing that the Bible has nothing to say against homosexuality, remind him gently that the evidence all points in the opposite direction. Just remember that there is probably very little to be gained by way of disputation.

On the whole, a case like this calls for generous amounts of patience and prayer.

In closing, we can't overemphasize the importance of

enlisting the help of a professional counselor.

If an adult child reveals his or her homosexuality, Christian parents should also make it clear that, no matter what, love and grace will triumph. As Christians, we are commanded to love one another despite our imperfections. First John 4:8 issues a stern warning to parents and children alike: "The one who does not love does not know God, because God is love" (HCSB).

More from God's Word

Every kingdom divided against itself is headed for destruction, and a house divided against itself falls.
LUKE 11:17 HCSB

You shall have no other gods before Me.
EXODUS 20:3 NKJV

Unless the LORD builds the house, they labor in vain who build it; unless the LORD guards the city, the watchman stays awake in vain.
PSALM 127:1 NKJV

Love must be without hypocrisy. Detest evil; cling to what is good. Show family affection to one another with brotherly love. Outdo one another in showing honor.
ROMANS 12:9–10 HCSB

Better a dry crust with peace than a house full of feasting with strife.
PROVERBS 17:1 HCSB

More Thoughts
about Christian Family Values

*A family is a place where principles
are hammered out and honed
on the anvil of everyday living.*

CHARLES SWINDOLL

*The family circle is the
supreme conductor of Christianity.*

HENRY DRUMMOND

*We believe all sins, including sexual sins,
must be pointed out as sinful,
inappropriate, and hurtful.*

FRANK PAGE

*Faith in Christ is the most important
of all principles in building a happy marriage
and a successful home.*

BILLY GRAHAM

13

The Question

Are people born gay, or is it a choice?

The Answer

Many factors contribute to a person's having homosexual feelings. However, no reliable studies have shown that people are "born gay."

Perhaps there is some genetic predisposition towards certain lifestyles. However, we still must recognize the reality of choice and the recognition that people are called upon to make mature decisions based on what scripture declares to be truth and right. God's Word is clear and His way is always right.

FRANK PAGE

Is It a Choice?

*The fear of the L*ORD *is the beginning of knowledge,*
but fools despise wisdom and discipline.

PROVERBS 1:7 NIV

Are people born gay? To date, no genetic marker has been discovered, but that fact doesn't necessarily mean that people consciously choose homosexuality. As Jeff Johnston, the Gender Issues Analyst for Focus on the Family, observed, "Most people do not overtly choose to have homosexual attractions, no more than anyone 'chooses' to be attracted to brunettes or people with green eyes. Studies and individual testimonies demonstrate there are a variety of roads into homosexuality, and the specific route is different for each person. Homosexuality probably results from a combination of factors, including (but not limited to) personality, relationships, trauma, developmental issues, and cultural influences. Some people with same-sex attractions are able to point to early childhood experiences or family dynamics that contributed to their feelings."

Even though people can't necessarily control their same-sex attractions, they can control how they respond to their sexual urges. As Johnston noted, "Choice becomes very important when a person is deciding how to handle same-sex attractions. Will they choose to seek the help of God and others to follow God's design for human sexual expression? Will they seek healing, forgiveness, and grace? Will they choose to place their confidence in and follow Jesus Christ? Those choices are significant, indeed, but they are the choices we all face."

So, if you're dealing with feelings of same-sex attraction, you're faced with a very important choice: to obey God or not.

The choice is straightforward, and the answer should be obvious. When you obey God, you'll experience a full measure of His abundance. When you disobey Him, you won't.

More from God's Word

*Now if any of you lacks wisdom,
he should ask God, who gives to all generously
and without criticizing, and it will be given to him.*
JAMES 1:5 NLT

*Who is wise and has understanding among you?
He should show his works by good conduct
with wisdom's gentleness.*
JAMES 3:13 HCSB

*So you may walk in the way of goodness, and keep
to the paths of righteousness. For the upright will
dwell in the land, and the blameless will remain in it.*
PROVERBS 2:20–21 NKJV

*A good man produces good out of the good
storeroom of his heart. An evil man produces evil
out of the evil storeroom, for his mouth speaks from
the overflow of the heart.*
LUKE 6:45 HCSB

*Blessed is the man who walks not in the counsel
of the ungodly, nor stands in the path of sinners,
nor sits in the seat of the scornful.*
PSALM 1:1 NKJV

More Thoughts
about Making Choices

*God always gives His very best
to those who leave the choice with Him.*

HUDSON TAYLOR

*Your little choices become habits that affect
the bigger decisions you make in life.*

ELIZABETH GEORGE

Every choice you make has an end result.

ZIG ZIGLAR

*No matter how many books you read, no matter
how many schools you attend, you're never really
wise until you start making wise choices.*

MARIE T. FREEMAN

*Men are free to decide their own moral choices,
but they are also under the necessity to account
to God for those choices.*

A. W. TOZER

14

The Question

A loved one is practicing a gay lifestyle,
and I can't seem to find it in my heart to forgive.
What does the Bible say about it?

The Answer

God's Word instructs you to forgive others,
no exceptions. Forgiveness is its own reward
and bitterness is its own punishment, so guard
your words and your thoughts accordingly.

*He who cannot forgive others breaks the bridge
over which he himself must pass.*

CORRIE ten BOOM

Forgiveness Now

And whenever you stand praying,
if you have anything against anyone,
forgive him, so that your Father in heaven
will also forgive you your wrongdoing.
MARK 11:25 HCSB

As Jesus of Nazareth hung on the cross, He sought forgiveness for those who tortured Him. Such is the nature of true forgiveness. Christ, like His heavenly Father, was merciful. And He instructs us to be merciful, too, in every situation, no matter how difficult.

Has a loved one chosen a lifestyle that breaks your heart? Have you experienced pain so intense that you fear your life will be forever changed? And do you blame your loved one for the sorrow you feel? If so, it's time to imitate Christ on the cross. It's time to forgive.

If, in your heart, you hold bitterness against even a single person, today is the day to show mercy and move on. Hatred and bitterness are not part of God's plan for your life. Forgiveness is.

More from God's Word

And be kind to one another,
tenderhearted, forgiving one another,
even as God in Christ forgave you.
EPHESIANS 4:32 NKJV

Judge not, and you shall not be judged.
Condemn not, and you shall not be condemned.
Forgive, and you will be forgiven.
LUKE 6:37 NKJV

Above all, love each other deeply,
because love covers over a multitude of sins.
1 PETER 4:8 NIV

But I say to you, love your enemies
and pray for those who persecute you.
MATTHEW 5:44 NASB

Blessed are the merciful,
for they will be shown mercy.
MATTHEW 5:7 NIV

More Thoughts about Forgiveness

Forgiveness does not change the past,
but it does enlarge the future.

DAVID JEREMIAH

One bold stroke, forgiveness obliterates the past
and permits us to enter the land of new beginnings.

BILLY GRAHAM

Forgiveness is an act of the will, and the will can
function regardless of the temperature of the heart.

CORRIE TEN BOOM

Forgiveness is one of the most beautiful words in
the human vocabulary. How much pain could be
avoided if we all learned the meaning of this word!

BILLY GRAHAM

Forgiveness is God's command.

MARTIN LUTHER

15

The Question

When I encounter people who are obviously gay, I don't know how to respond. What should I do?

The Answer

As a follower of Christ, you must try your best to treat others as He would.

Be assured, if you walk with Him and look to Him and expect help from Him, He will never fail you.

GEORGE MÜLLER

Following Christ

*Then He said to them all, "If anyone wants
to come with Me, he must deny himself,
take up his cross daily, and follow Me."*
LUKE 9:23 HCSB

If you're not sure how to treat another person, ask yourself this
simple question: "How would Jesus meet and treat this person?"
Then you'll know precisely what to do.

Every day, we're presented with countless opportunities to
honor God by following in the footsteps of His Son. But we're
sorely tempted to do otherwise. The world is filled to the brim
with temptations and distractions that beckon us down a different path. Elisabeth Elliot had this advice for believers everywhere: "Choose Jesus Christ! Deny yourself, take up the cross,
and follow Him, for the world must be shown. The world must
see, in us, a discernible, visible, startling difference."

Today, treat everyone you meet with kindness, with cour-
tesy, and with love. Do your part to take up the cross and follow
your Savior, even if the world encourages you to do otherwise.
When you're traveling step-by-step with the Son of God, you're
always on the right path.

More from God's Word

*But whoever keeps His word, truly in him the love
of God is perfected. This is how we know we are
in Him: The one who says he remains in Him
should walk just as He walked.*

1 John 2:5–6 HCSB

*Walk in a manner worthy of the God
who calls you into His own kingdom and glory.*

1 Thessalonians 2:12 NASB

For we walk by faith, not by sight.

2 Corinthians 5:7 HCSB

*Take my yoke upon you, and learn of me; for I am
meek and lowly in heart: and ye shall find rest unto
your souls. For my yoke is easy, and my burden is light.*

Matthew 11:29–30 KJV

*Whoever is not willing to carry the cross and follow
me is not worthy of me. Those who try to hold on to
their lives will give up true life. Those who give up
their lives for me will hold on to true life.*

Matthew 10:38–39 NCV

More Thoughts
about Following Christ

The crucial question for each of us is this:
what do you think of Jesus, and do you yet
have a personal acquaintance with Him?

HANNAH WHITALL SMITH

Choose Jesus Christ! Deny yourself, take up the
cross, and follow Him, for the world must be shown.
The world must see, in us, a discernible, visible,
startling difference.

ELISABETH ELLIOT

Christ is not valued at all unless
He is valued above all.

ST. AUGUSTINE

As you walk through the valley of the unknown,
you will find the footprints of Jesus both in front
of you and beside you.

CHARLES STANLEY

The beautiful thing about this adventure
called faith is that we can count on Him
never to lead us astray.

CHARLES SWINDOLL

16

The Question

The world seems to be such a confusing place.
Sometimes I honestly don't know what's right
and what's wrong. What should I do?

The Answer

When you're concerned or confused,
turn first to God. He has promised to guide you,
and He will never lead you astray.

*God never leads us to do anything
that is contrary to the Bible.*

BILLY GRAHAM

Seek God's Guidance

Trust in the LORD with all your heart, and lean not on your own understanding; in all your ways acknowledge Him, and He shall direct your paths.

PROVERBS 3:5–6 NKJV

If you're struggling with your own sexuality, or if you're concerned about the sexual preferences of a loved one, you should talk to God about it. When you ask for God's guidance, with your heart and mind open to His direction, He will lead you along a path of His choosing. But for many of us, listening to God is hard. We have so many things we want, and so many needs to pray for, that we spend far more time talking at God than we do listening to Him.

Corrie ten Boom observed, "God's guidance is even more important than common sense. I can declare that the deepest darkness is outshone by the light of Jesus." These words remind us that life is best lived when we seek the Lord's direction early and often.

Our Father has many ways to make Himself known. Our challenge is to make ourselves open to His instruction. So if you're unsure of your next step, trust God's promises and talk to Him often. When you do, He'll guide your steps today, tomorrow, and forever.

More from God's Word

Morning by morning he wakens me and opens my understanding to his will. The Sovereign L<small>ORD</small> has spoken to me, and I have listened.

I<small>SAIAH</small> 50:4–5 NLT

Yet L<small>ORD</small>, You are our Father; we are the clay, and You are our potter; we all are the work of Your hands.

I<small>SAIAH</small> 64:8 HCSB

The L<small>ORD</small> says, "I will guide you along the best pathway for your life. I will advise you and watch over you."

P<small>SALM</small> 32:8 NLT

Teach me to do Your will, for You are my God; Your Spirit is good. Lead me in the land of uprightness.

P<small>SALM</small> 143:10 NKJV

Shew me thy ways, O L<small>ORD</small>; teach me thy paths. Lead me in thy truth, and teach me: for thou art the God of my salvation; on thee do I wait all the day.

P<small>SALM</small> 25:4–5 KJV

More Thoughts
about God's Guidance

When we are obedient,
God guides our steps and our stops.

CORRIE TEN BOOM

Are you serious about wanting God's guidance to
become a personal reality in your life? The first step
is to tell God that you know you can't manage
your own life; that you need His help.

CATHERINE MARSHALL

The will of God will never take us
where the grace of God cannot sustain us.

BILLY GRAHAM

As you walk through the valley of the unknown,
you will find the footprints of Jesus both in front
of you and beside you.

CHARLES STANLEY

We should not be upset when unexpected and
upsetting things happen. God, in His wisdom,
means to make something of us which we have
not yet attained and is dealing with us accordingly.

J. I. PACKER

17

The Question

I'm concerned about someone who doesn't seem to want my help. What can I do?

The Answer

Sometimes the only thing you can do is to pray for that person.

It is impossible to overstate the need for prayer in the fabric of family life.

JAMES DOBSON

Pray About It

I desire therefore that the men pray everywhere,
lifting up holy hands, without wrath and doubting.
1 TIMOTHY 2:8 NKJV

If you're serious about changing your lifestyle, prayer is a powerful tool that you can use to revolutionize your life and transform yourself. And if you're concerned about a loved one who's chosen a gay lifestyle, prayer is the perfect way to petition your Creator.

God hears every prayer and responds in His own way and according to His own timetable. When you make a habit of consulting Him about everything, He'll guide you along a path of His choosing, which, by the way, is the path you should take. And when you petition Him for strength, He'll give you the courage to face any problem and the power to meet any challenge.

So today, instead of turning things over in your mind, turn them over to God in prayer. Take your concerns to the Lord and leave them there. Your heavenly Father is listening, and He wants to hear from you. Now.

More from God's Word

Is anyone among you suffering? He should pray.
JAMES 5:13 HCSB

Confess your trespasses to one another, and pray for one another, that you may be healed. The effective, fervent prayer of a righteous man avails much.
JAMES 5:16 NKJV

And whenever you stand praying, if you have anything against anyone, forgive him, so that your Father in heaven will also forgive you your wrongdoing.
MARK 11:25 HCSB

Ask, and it will be given to you; seek, and you will find; knock, and it will be opened to you. For everyone who asks receives, and he who seeks finds, and to him who knocks it shall be opened.
MATTHEW 7:7-8 NASB

Rejoice always, pray without ceasing, in everything give thanks; for this is the will of God in Christ Jesus for you.
1 THESSALONIANS 5:16-18 NKJV

More Thoughts about Prayer

Prayer is our lifeline to God.
BILLY GRAHAM

*Two wings are necessary to lift our souls
toward God: prayer and praise. Prayer asks.
Praise accepts the answer.*
LETTIE COWMAN

*Don't pray when you feel like it. Have
an appointment with the Lord and keep it.*
CORRIE TEN BOOM

*It is impossible to overstate the need
for prayer in the fabric of family life.*
JAMES DOBSON

God's solution is just a prayer away!
MAX LUCADO

18

The Question

I've done things I'm not proud of.
In fact, I'm very ashamed about some
of the things I've done. What should I do?

The Answer

First, be certain that you're no longer doing the
thing that caused your guilt in the first place. Then,
ask for forgiveness (from God and from anybody
you've hurt). Next, make sure you forgive yourself.
And finally, if you still have residual feelings of
bitterness or regret, keep asking God to heal your
heart. When you ask, He will answer in His own
time and in His own way.

*The purpose of guilt is to bring us to Jesus.
Once we are there, then its purpose is finished.
If we continue to make ourselves guilty—
to blame ourselves—then that is a sin in itself.*

CORRIE TEN BOOM

Beyond Guilt

It is I who sweep away your transgressions for My own sake and remember your sins no more.
ISAIAH 43:25 HCSB

All of us have sinned. We've all made countless mistakes and fallen short of the mark on too many occasions to count. Sometimes our sins result from our own stubborn rebellion against God's commandments. And sometimes we are swept up in events that are beyond our ability to control. Under either set of circumstances, we may experience intense feelings of guilt. But God has an answer for the guilt we feel. That answer, of course, is His forgiveness.

When we confess our wrongdoings and repent from them, we are forgiven by the One who created us. Genuine repentance requires more than simply offering God apologies for our misdeeds. Real repentance may start with feelings of sorrow and remorse, but it ends only when we turn away from the sin that has heretofore distanced us from our Creator. In truth, we offer our most meaningful apologies to God not with our words, but with our actions. As long as we are still engaged in sin, we may be "repenting," but we have not fully "repented."

Are you troubled by feelings of guilt or regret? If so, you must first repent from your misdeeds, and you must ask your heavenly Father for His forgiveness. When you do so, He will forgive you completely and without reservation. Then you must forgive yourself just as God has forgiven you: thoroughly, unconditionally, and eternally.

More from God's Word

Be gracious to me, God, according to Your faithful love; according to Your abundant compassion, blot out my rebellion. Wash away my guilt and cleanse me from my sin.

PSALM 51:1–2 HCSB

Let us come near to God with a sincere heart and a sure faith, because we have been made free from a guilty conscience, and our bodies have been washed with pure water.

HEBREWS 10:22 NCV

How can I know all the sins lurking in my heart? Cleanse me from these hidden faults. Keep your servant from deliberate sins! Don't let them control me. Then I will be free of guilt and innocent of great sin.

PSALM 19:12–13 NLT

Create in me a pure heart, God, and make my spirit right again.

PSALM 51:10 NCV

Consider my affliction and rescue me, for I have not forgotten Your instruction.

PSALM 119:153 HCSB

More Thoughts
about Guilt and Forgiveness

*The redemption, accomplished for us by our Lord
Jesus Christ on the cross at Calvary, is redemption
from the power of sin as well as from its guilt. Christ
is able to save all who come unto God by Him.*

HANNAH WHITALL SMITH

*Guilt is an appalling waste of energy; you can't
build on it. It's only good for wallowing in.*

KATHERINE MANSFIELD

*God's mercy is boundless, free,
and, through Jesus Christ our Lord,
available to us in our present situation.*

A. W. TOZER

*The most marvelous ingredient in the forgiveness
of God is that He also forgets, the one thing
a human being cannot do. With God, forgetting
is a divine attribute. God's forgiveness forgets.*

OSWALD CHAMBERS

*God does not wish us to remember
what He is willing to forget.*

GEORGE A. BUTTRICK

19

The Question

I have a loved one who claims to be gay, and I'm very worried. When I'm overcome by anxiety and fear, what should I do? And where should I turn?

The Answer

Carefully divide your areas of concern into two categories: things you can control and those you cannot control. Once you've done so, spend your time working to resolve the things you can control, and entrust everything else to God.

Do not worry about tomorrow.
This is not a suggestion, but a command.

SARAH YOUNG

Beyond Worry

Therefore do not worry about tomorrow,
for tomorrow will worry about its own things.
Sufficient for the day is its own trouble.
MATTHEW 6:34 NKJV

Because we are human beings who have the capacity to think and to anticipate future events, we worry. We worry about big things, little things, and just about everything in between. To make matters worse, we live in a world that breeds anxiety and fosters fear. So it's not surprising that when we come face-to-face with tough times or difficult decisions, we may fall prey to discouragement, doubt, or depression. But our Father in heaven has other plans.

God has promised that we can lead lives of abundance, not anxiety. In fact, His Word instructs us to "be anxious for nothing" (Philippians 4:6 NKJV). But how can we put our fears to rest? By taking those fears to Him and leaving them there.

The very same God who created the universe has promised to protect you now and forever. So what do you have to worry about? With God on your side, the answer is "nothing."

More from God's Word

*Peace I leave with you; My peace I give to you;
not as the world gives do I give to you. Do not let
your heart be troubled, nor let it be fearful.*
JOHN 14:27 NASB

*Do not be anxious about anything, but in every
situation, by prayer and petition, with thanksgiving,
present your requests to God.*
PHILIPPIANS 4:6 NIV

*Let not your heart be troubled;
you believe in God, believe also in Me.*
JOHN 14:1 NKJV

*Cast all your anxiety on him
because he cares for you.*
1 PETER 5:7 NIV

*Cast your burden on the LORD,
and He shall sustain you; He shall never
permit the righteous to be moved.*
PSALM 55:22 NKJV

More Thoughts
about Anxiety and Worry

*It is not the cares of today, but the cares of
tomorrow, that weigh a man down. For the needs
of today we have corresponding strength given.
It is when tomorrow's burden is added to the burden
of today that the weight is more than we can bear.*

GEORGE MACDONALD

*Worry is the senseless process of cluttering up
tomorrow's opportunities with leftover
problems from today.*

BARBARA JOHNSON

*Tomorrow is busy worrying about itself;
don't get tangled up in its worry-webs.*

SARAH YOUNG

Pray, and let God worry.

MARTIN LUTHER

*Claim all of God's promises in the Bible.
Your sins, your worries, your life—
you may cast them all on Him.*

CORRIE TEN BOOM

20

The Question

The world keeps sending messages
that the gay lifestyle and gay marriage are okay.
But the Bible says otherwise. Is it possible that
the Bible is simply out of date?

The Answer

The Bible is never out of date. God's Word
is eternal and unchanging. No matter what
popular culture says, you must always trust God.

—⁓—

*Our first commitment is to God and His Word—
nothing else and no one else.*
RONNIE FLOYD

Trust His Voice,
Trust His Heart

*Trust in the LORD with all your heart, and lean not
on your own understanding; in all your ways
acknowledge Him, and He shall direct your paths.*

<small>PROVERBS 3:5–6 NKJV</small>

As we pass through this world, we travel past peaks and valleys. When we reach the mountaintops of life, we find it easy to praise God and to give thanks. And as we reach the crest of the mountain's peak, we find it easy to trust God's plan. But when we find ourselves in the dark valleys of life, when we face disappointment, despair, or heartbreak, it's much more difficult to trust God. Yet trust Him we must.

As Christians, we can be comforted: Whether we find ourselves at the pinnacle of the mountain or the darkest depths of the valley, God is there. And we Christians have every reason to live courageously. After all, Christ has already won the ultimate battle on the cross at Calvary.

So the next time you find your faith tested to the limit, lean upon God's promises. Trust His Son. Remember that God is always near and that He is your protector and your deliverer. When you are worried, anxious, or afraid, call upon Him. God can handle your problems infinitely better than you can, so turn them over to Him. Remember that God rules both mountaintops and valleys—with limitless wisdom and love—now and forever.

More from God's Word

The LORD is my rock, my fortress, and my deliverer,
my God, my mountain where I seek refuge.
My shield, the horn of my salvation,
my stronghold, my refuge, and my Savior.
2 SAMUEL 22:2–3 HCSB

Jesus said, "Don't let your hearts be troubled.
Trust in God, and trust in me."
JOHN 14:1 NCV

Those who trust in the LORD are like Mount Zion.
It cannot be shaken; it remains forever.
PSALM 125:1 HCSB

In quietness and trust is your strength.
ISAIAH 30:15 NASB

The fear of man is a snare, but the one
who trusts in the LORD is protected.
PROVERBS 29:25 HCSB

More Thoughts about Trusting God

One of the marks of spiritual maturity is the quiet confidence that God is in control, without the need to understand why He does what He does.

CHARLES SWINDOLL

When a train goes through a tunnel and it gets dark, you don't throw away your ticket and jump off. You sit still and trust the engineer.

CORRIE TEN BOOM

When trust is perfect and there is no doubt, prayer is simply the outstretched hand ready to receive.

E. M. BOUNDS

Never yield to gloomy anticipation.
Place your hope and confidence in God.
He has no record of failure.

LETTIE COWMAN

Never be afraid to trust an unknown future to a known God.

CORRIE TEN BOOM

21

The Question

I've done many things that I'm not proud of.
Lately it seems like I'm always focused on the past.
What should I do?

The Answer

If you're recovering from bad choices or difficult
circumstances, it's natural to spend time reliving
the past. But you shouldn't allow yourself
to become stuck there.

—⦚—

*Don't waste energy regretting the way things
are or thinking about what might have been.
Start at the present moment—accepting things
exactly as they are—and search for My way
in the midst of those circumstances.*

SARAH YOUNG

Making Peace with the Past

Do not remember the former things, nor consider the things of old. Behold, I will do a new thing.

Isaiah 43:18–19 NKJV

Since we can't change the mistakes and disappointments of the past, why do so many of us insist upon replaying them in our minds? Perhaps it's because we can't find it in our hearts to forgive the people who have harmed us or to move beyond the losses that we've suffered.

Reinhold Niebuhr composed a simple verse that came to be known as the Serenity Prayer: "God, grant me the serenity to accept the things I cannot change, the courage to change the things I can, and the wisdom to know the difference." Obviously, we cannot change the past. It is what it was and forever will be. The present, of course, is a different matter.

Can you summon both the courage and the wisdom to accept your past, accept God's forgiveness, and move on with your life? Can you accept the reality that yesterday—and all the yesterdays before it—are gone? And can you entrust all those yesterdays to God? Hopefully you can.

Today is filled with opportunities to obey God, to love your neighbors, to work, to play, and to celebrate life. If you sincerely wish to build a better tomorrow, you can start building it today. So, if you've endured a painful loss or a difficult past, accept it, learn from it, and forgive everybody, including yourself. Once you've made peace with your past, don't spend too much time there. Instead, live in the precious present, where opportunities abound and change is still possible.

More from God's Word

*He restoreth my soul: he leadeth me in the paths
of righteousness for his name's sake.*
PSALM 23:3 KJV

*Have mercy on me, O God, according to your
unfailing love; according to your great compassion
blot out my transgressions. Wash away all my
iniquity and cleanse me from my sin.*
PSALM 51:1–2 NIV

*And He who sits on the throne said,
"Behold, I am making all things new."*
REVELATION 21:5 NASB

*One thing I do, forgetting those things which
are behind and reaching forward to those things
which are ahead, I press toward the goal for the
prize of the upward call of God in Christ Jesus.*
PHILIPPIANS 3:13–14 NKJV

*Your old sinful self has died,
and your new life is kept with Christ in God.*
COLOSSIANS 3:3 NCV

More Thoughts
about Dealing with the Past

Trust the past to God's mercy, the present to God's love, and the future to God's providence.

St. Augustine

One bold stroke, forgiveness obliterates the past and permits us to enter the land of new beginnings.

Billy Graham

Who you are in Christ is far more important and meaningful than whatever has taken place in your past.

Elizabeth George

Don't be bound by the past and its failures. But don't forgets its lessons either.

Billy Graham

Acrid bitterness inevitably seeps into the lives of people who harbor grudges and suppress anger, and bitterness is always a poison. It keeps your pain alive instead of letting you deal with it and get beyond it.

Lee Strobel

22

The Question

I've been praying for God's guidance and His help. But it seems like nothing has happened yet. What does the Bible say about that?

The Answer

You should always trust God's timing, and you should wait patiently for His plans to unfold. God's plans are best. Trust Him.

We must learn to move according to the timetable of the Timeless One, and to be at peace.

ELISABETH ELLIOT

Trust God's Timing

Therefore humble yourselves under the mighty hand of God, that He may exalt you in due time.
1 PETER 5:6 NKJV

If you're trying to resolve personal issues, or if you're trying to help a loved one who's in trouble, you're in a hurry. You know precisely what you want, and you know precisely when you want it: as soon as possible. Because your time on earth is limited, you may feel a sense of urgency. God does not. There is no panic in heaven.

Our heavenly Father, in His infinite wisdom, operates according to His own timetable, not ours. He has plans that we cannot see and purposes that we cannot know. He has created a world that unfolds according to His own schedule. Thank goodness! After all, He is omniscient; He is trustworthy; and He knows what's best for us.

If you've been waiting impatiently for the Lord to answer your prayers, it's time to put a stop to all that needless worry. You can be sure that God will answer your prayers when the time is right. You job is to keep praying—and working—until He does.

More from God's Word

Those who trust in the LORD are like Mount Zion.
It cannot be shaken; it remains forever.
PSALM 125:1 HCSB

To every thing there is a season,
and a time to every purpose under the heaven.
ECCLESIASTES 3:1 KJV

Trust in the Lord with all your heart, and lean
not on your own understanding; in all your ways
acknowledge Him, and He shall direct your paths.
PROVERBS 3:5–6 NKJV

He has made everything appropriate in its time.
He has also put eternity in their hearts,
but man cannot discover the work
God has done from beginning to end.
ECCLESIASTES 3:11 HCSB

Yet the LORD longs to be gracious to you;
therefore he will rise up to show you compassion.
For the LORD is a God of justice.
Blessed are all who wait for him!
ISAIAH 30:18 NIV

More Thoughts
about God's Timing

Waiting on God brings us to the journey's end quicker than our feet.

LETTIE COWMAN

We often hear about waiting on God, which actually means that He is waiting until we are ready. There is another side, however. When we wait for God, we are waiting until He is ready.

LETTIE COWMAN

We must learn to move according to the timetable of the Timeless One, and to be at peace.

ELISABETH ELLIOT

Teach us, O Lord, the disciplines of patience, for to wait is often harder than to work.

PETER MARSHALL

The Christian's journey through life isn't a sprint but a marathon.

BILLY GRAHAM

23

The Question

From a moral standpoint, the world seems to be spinning out of control. How can I find a minute's peace?

The Answer

To keep your moral footing, you should be spending time with God each day. You need to be still and listen to God. He has something important to say to you. When you listen to Him, you'll be blessed.

God's voice is still and quiet and easily buried under an avalanche of clamor.

CHARLES STANLEY

He Speaks in Quiet

Listen in silence before me.
Isaiah 41:1 NLT

Jesus understood the importance of silence. He spent precious hours alone with God, and so should we. But with our busy schedules, we're tempted to rush from place to place, checking smartphones along the way, leaving no time to contemplate spiritual matters.

You live in a noisy world, a complicated society where sights and sounds surround you and silence is in short supply. Everywhere you turn, or so it seems, the media seeks to grab your attention and hijack your thoughts. You're surrounded by big screens and little ones. And your phone can keep you logged in day and night if you let it. Don't let it.

Today and every day, you need quiet, uninterrupted time alone with God. You need to be still and listen for His voice. And you need to seek His guidance in matters great and small. Your Creator has important plans for your day and your life. And He's trying to get His message through. You owe it to Him—and to yourself—to listen and to learn in silence.

More from God's Word

Be still, and know that I am God.
PSALM 46:10 KJV

To every thing there is a season…
a time to keep silence, and a time to speak.
ECCLESIASTES 3:1, 7 KJV

In quietness and in confidence
shall be your strength.
ISAIAH 30:15 KJV

Truly my soul silently waits for God;
from Him comes my salvation.
PSALM 62:1 NKJV

Now in the morning, having risen a long while
before daylight, He went out and departed
to a solitary place; and there He prayed.
MARK 1:35 NKJV

More Thoughts about Quiet Time

*Strength is found not in busyness
and noise but in quietness.*

LETTIE COWMAN

*The world is full of noise. Might we not set ourselves
to learn silence, stillness, solitude?*

ELISABETH ELLIOT

Nothing in all creation is so like God as stillness.

JOHANN WOLFGANG VON GOETHE

*Fold the arms of your faith and wait in quietness
until the light goes up in your darkness.*

GEORGE MACDONALD

*I don't see how any Christian can survive,
let alone live life as more than a conqueror,
apart from a quiet time alone with God.*

KAY ARTHUR

24

The Question

The Bible talks about peace,
but I can't seem to find it.
What should I do?

The Answer

God's peace surpasses human understanding.
When we accept His peace, it revolutionizes our
lives. When we call upon Him, He can restore our
souls. But if we're living in outright rebellion against
God, we can't expect to experience the peace
that He promises to those who obey Him.

*Prayer guards hearts and minds and causes God
to bring peace out of chaos.*
BETH MOORE

Seek God's Peace

Peace I leave with you, My peace I give to you;
not as the world gives do I give to you. Let not your
heart be troubled, neither let it be afraid.

JOHN 14:27 NKJV

Peace. It's such a beautiful word. It conveys images of serenity, contentment, and freedom from the trials and tribulations of everyday existence. Peace means freedom from conflict, freedom from inner turmoil, and freedom from worry. Peace is such a beautiful concept that modern media and marketers attempt to sell it by promoting the idea that any behavior is acceptable "if it doesn't hurt other people." But despite claims to the contrary, real peace isn't the result of self-gratification. It's the result of honoring God and following His Son.

Have you discovered the genuine peace that can be yours through Christ? Or are you still scurrying after the illusion of peace that the world promises but cannot deliver? If you've turned things over to Jesus, you'll be blessed now and forever. So what are you waiting for? Let Him rule your heart and your thoughts, beginning now. When you do, you'll experience the peace that only He can give.

More from God's Word

The peace of God, which passeth all understanding, shall keep your hearts and minds through Christ Jesus.

PHILIPPIANS 4:7 KJV

These things I have spoken to you, that in Me you may have peace. In the world you will have tribulation; but be of good cheer, I have overcome the world.

JOHN 16:33 NKJV

But the fruit of the Spirit is love, joy, peace, patience, kindness, goodness, faith, gentleness, self-control. Against such things there is no law.

GALATIANS 5:22–23 HCSB

"I will give peace, real peace, to those far and near, and I will heal them," says the LORD.

ISAIAH 57:19 NCV

He Himself is our peace.

EPHESIANS 2:14 NASB

More Thoughts about Peace

*Peace does not mean to be in a place
where there is no noise, trouble, or hard work.
Peace means to be in the midst of all those things
and still be calm in your heart.*

CATHERINE MARSHALL

*God's power is great enough for our deepest
desperation. You can go on. You can pick up the
pieces and start anew. You can face your fears.
You can find peace in the rubble. There is healing
for your soul.*

SUZANNE DALE EZELL

*Deep within the center of the soul is a chamber
of peace where God lives and where, if we will
enter it and quiet all the other sounds,
we can hear His gentle whisper.*

LETTIE COWMAN

*In the center of a hurricane there is absolute quiet
and peace. There is no safer place than in the
center of the will of God.*

CORRIE TEN BOOM

*Only Christ can meet the deepest needs of our world
and our hearts. Christ alone can bring lasting peace.*

BILLY GRAHAM

25

The Question

I can talk to God, but I have trouble waiting for His answers. What does the Bible say about listening to God?

The Answer

Whether you are communicating with God or with other people, the Bible reminds us time and again that it's always a good idea to listen more than you talk.

The purpose of all prayer is to find God's will and to make that our prayer.

CATHERINE MARSHALL

Be Still and Listen

Be still, and know that I am God.
PSALM 46:10 KJV

God speaks to us in different ways at different times. Sometimes He speaks loudly and clearly. But more often He speaks in a quiet voice—and if you are wise, you will be listening carefully when He does. To do so, you must carve out quiet moments each day to study His Word and to sense His direction.

Are you willing to pray sincerely and then to wait quietly for God's response? Can you quiet yourself long enough to listen to your conscience? Are you attuned to the subtle guidance of your intuition? Hopefully so. Usually God refrains from sending His messages on stone tablets or city billboards. More often He communicates in subtler ways. If you sincerely desire to hear His voice, you must listen carefully, and you must do so in the silent corners of your quiet, willing heart.

More from God's Word

Rest in the LORD, and wait patiently for Him.
PSALM 37:7 NKJV

Be silent before Me.
ISAIAH 41:1 HCSB

The one who is from God listens to God's words.
This is why you don't listen,
because you are not from God.
JOHN 8:47 HCSB

In quietness and in confidence
shall be your strength.
ISAIAH 30:15 KJV

Listen, listen to me, and eat what is good,
and you will delight in the richest of fare.
Give ear and come to me;
listen, that you may live.
ISAIAH 55:2–3 NIV

More Thoughts
about Listening to God

*When God speaks to us,
He should have our full attention.*

BILLY GRAHAM

*God's voice is still and quiet and easily buried
under an avalanche of clamor.*

CHARLES STANLEY

*Prayer is not monologue, but dialogue. God's voice
in response to mine is its most essential part.*

ANDREW MURRAY

*Deep within the center of the soul is a chamber
of peace where God lives and where, if we will
enter it and quiet all the other sounds,
we can hear His gentle whisper.*

LETTIE COWMAN

*If you, too, will learn to wait upon God, to get alone
with Him, and remain silent so that you can hear
His voice when He is ready to speak to you,
what a difference it will make in your life!*

KAY ARTHUR

26

The Question

It's hard not to be judgmental of other people, especially people whose choices I don't endorse. And it's hard not to judge their motives. What does the Bible say about judging others?

The Answer

You must make judgments about people's behaviors, as well as your own, using God's Word as your reference. But God's Word warns against judging other people. Your ability to judge others requires a divine insight that you simply don't have. So do everybody (including yourself) a favor: don't judge.

Speak and act as those who will be judged by the law of freedom. For judgment is without mercy to the one who hasn't shown mercy. Mercy triumphs over judgment.

JAMES 2:12–13 HCSB

Let God Be the Judge

Judge not, and you shall not be judged.
Condemn not, and you shall not be condemned.
Forgive, and you will be forgiven.

LUKE 6:37 NKJV

We mortals feel compelled to serve as informal judges and juries, pronouncing our own verdicts on the actions and perceived motivations of others, all the while excusing—or oftentimes hiding—our own shortcomings. But God's Word instructs us to let Him be the judge. He knows that we, with our limited knowledge and personal biases, are simply ill-equipped to assess the actions of others. The act of judging, then, becomes not only an act of futility but also an affront to our Creator.

When Jesus came upon a woman who had been condemned by the Pharisees, He spoke not only to the people who had gathered there but also to all generations to come. Christ warned, "He that is without sin among you, let him first cast a stone at her" (John 8:7 KJV). The message is clear: because we are all sinners, we must refrain from the temptation to judge others.

So the next time you're tempted to cast judgment on another human being, resist that temptation. God hasn't called you to be a judge; He's called you to be a witness.

More from God's Word

Don't criticize one another, brothers. He who criticizes a brother or judges his brother criticizes the law and judges the law. But if you judge the law, you are not a doer of the law but a judge.
JAMES 4:11 HCSB

Therefore, any one of you who judges is without excuse. For when you judge another, you condemn yourself, since you, the judge, do the same things.
ROMANS 2:1 HCSB

Do everything without grumbling and arguing, so that you may be blameless and pure.
PHILIPPIANS 2:14–15 HCSB

Those who guard their lips preserve their lives, but those who speak rashly will come to ruin.
PROVERBS 13:3 NIV

Let the words of my mouth and the meditation of my heart be acceptable in Your sight, O LORD, my strength and my Redeemer.
PSALM 19:14 NKJV

More Thoughts about Judging Others

Judging draws the judgment of others.

CATHERINE MARSHALL

*We must learn to regard people less
in the light of what they do or omit to do,
and more in light of what they suffer.*

DIETRICH BONHOEFFER

*Don't judge other people more harshly
than you want God to judge you.*

MARIE T. FREEMAN

*Yes, let God be the Judge.
Your job today is to be a witness.*

WARREN WIERSBE

*Oh, how horrible our sins look when they
are committed by someone else.*

CHARLES SWINDOLL

27

The Question

My views on homosexuality are driving a wedge between my loved ones and me. I'm bitter about it. Why is it important for me to overcome feelings of bitterness?

The Answer

Until you can forgive others, you'll be trapped in an emotional prison of your own making.

*Resentment always hurts you
more than the person you resent.*

RICK WARREN

Bitterness:
Beware of the Poison

He who says he is in the light,
and hates his brother, is in darkness until now.
1 John 2:9 NKJV

Bitterness is a spiritual sickness. It will consume your soul; it is dangerous to your emotional health; it can destroy you if you let it. So don't let it!

The world holds few if any rewards for those who remain angrily focused upon the past. Still, the act of forgiveness is difficult for all but the most saintly men and women. Being frail, fallible, imperfect human beings, most of us are quick to anger, quick to blame, slow to forgive, and even slower to forget. Yet we know that it's best to forgive others, just as we, too, have been forgiven.

If there exists even one person—including yourself—against whom you still harbor bitter feelings, it's time to forgive and move on. Bitterness and regret are not part of God's plan for you, but God won't force you to forgive others. It's a job that only you can finish, and the sooner you finish it, the better.

If you are caught up in intense feelings of anger or resentment, you know all too well the destructive power of these emotions. How can you rid yourself of these feelings? First you must prayerfully ask God to cleanse your heart. Then you must learn to catch yourself whenever thoughts of bitterness or hatred begin to attack you. Your challenge is this: You must learn to resist negative thoughts before they hijack your emotions. When you learn to direct your thoughts toward more positive topics, you'll be protected from the spiritual and emotional consequences of bitterness...and you'll be wiser, healthier, and happier, too.

More from God's Word

*You have heard that it was said, "Love your
neighbor and hate your enemy." But I tell you,
love your enemies and pray for those
who persecute you, that you may
be children of your Father in heaven.*

MATTHEW 5:43–45 NIV

*My dear brothers and sisters, always be willing
to listen and slow to speak. Do not become angry
easily, because anger will not help you live the right
kind of life God wants.*

JAMES 1:19–20 NCV

*If anyone says, "I am living in the light,"
but hates a Christian brother or sister,
that person is still living in darkness.*

1 JOHN 2:9 NLT

*Everyone must be quick to hear, slow to speak,
and slow to anger, for man's anger does not
accomplish God's righteousness.*

JAMES 1:19–20 HCSB

*Do not be conquered by evil,
but conquer evil with good.*

ROMANS 12:21 HCSB

More Thoughts about Bitterness

*He who cannot forgive others breaks the bridge
over which he himself must pass.*

CORRIE TEN BOOM

*Bitterness is a spiritual cancer, a rapidly growing
malignancy that can consume your life. Bitterness
cannot be ignored but must be healed at the very
core, and only Christ can heal bitterness.*

BETH MOORE

Bitterness imprisons life; love releases it.

HARRY EMERSON FOSDICK

*Bitterness is anger gone sour,
an attitude of deep discontent that poisons
our souls and destroys our peace.*

BILLY GRAHAM

*Revenge easily descends into an endless cycle
of hate and violence. The Bible says never
repay evil with evil.*

BILLY GRAHAM

28

The Question

Sometimes I feel stuck, and sometimes I feel confused. How can I discover God's purpose for my life?

The Answer

God's plans for you are unfolding day by day. If you keep your eyes and your heart open, He'll reveal those plans. God has big things in store for you, but He may have quite a few lessons to teach you before you are fully prepared to do His will and fulfill His purposes.

You will show me the path of life;
in Your presence is fullness of joy;
at Your right hand are pleasures forevermore.
PSALM 16:11 NKJV

Discovering Your Purpose

We have also received an inheritance in Him, predestined according to the purpose of the One who works out everything in agreement with the decision of His will.

EPHESIANS 1:11 HCSB

God doesn't do things by accident. He didn't put you here by chance. The Lord didn't deliver you to your particular place, at this particular time, with your particular set of talents and opportunities on a whim. He has a plan, a one-of-a-kind mission designed especially for you. Discovering that plan may take time. But if you keep asking God for guidance, He'll lead you along a path of His choosing and give you every tool you need to fulfill His will.

Of course, you'll probably encounter a few impediments as you attempt to discover the exact nature of God's purpose for your life. And you may travel a few dead ends along the way. But if you keep searching, and if you genuinely seek the Lord's guidance, He'll reveal His plans at a time and place of His own choosing.

Today and every day, God is beckoning you to hear His voice and follow His plan for your life. When you listen—and when you answer His call—you'll be amazed at the wonderful things that an all-knowing, all-powerful God can do.

More from God's Word

We must do the works of Him who sent Me while it is day. Night is coming when no one can work.
JOHN 9:4 HCSB

And whatever you do, do it heartily, as to the Lord and not to men.
COLOSSIANS 3:23 NKJV

For we are His creation, created in Christ Jesus for good works, which God prepared ahead of time so that we should walk in them.
EPHESIANS 2:10 HCSB

For we are God's coworkers. You are God's field, God's building.
1 CORINTHIANS 3:9 HCSB

Whether you eat or drink, or whatever you do, do it all for the glory of God.
1 CORINTHIANS 10:31 NLT

More Thoughts about Purpose

All of God's people are ordinary people
who have been made extraordinary
by the purpose He has given them.

OSWALD CHAMBERS

The easiest way to discover the purpose
of an invention is to ask the creator of it. The same
is true for discovering your life's purpose: ask God.

RICK WARREN

There's some task which the God of all the universe,
the great Creator, has for you to do, and which will
remain undone and incomplete until by faith and
obedience you step into the will of God.

ALAN REDPATH

You weren't an accident. You weren't mass
produced. You aren't an assembly-line product.
You were deliberately planned, specifically gifted,
and lovingly positioned on the Earth
by the Master Craftsman.

MAX LUCADO

Live out your life in its full meaning; it is God's life.

JOSIAH ROYCE

29

The Question

Does God love homosexuals?

The Answer

Homosexual behavior is sinful, but it is not an unforgivable sin. All of us have sinned, and God still loves us, just as He loves homosexuals.

God's love is unchangeable. He knows exactly what we are and loves us anyway.

BILLY GRAHAM

For God So Loved
the World...

For God so loved the world, that he gave his only begotten Son, that whosoever believeth in him should not perish, but have everlasting life.

JOHN 3:16 KJV

Does God love homosexuals? Of course He does. All of us have sinned, and while God does not love our sins, He does love sinners.

Does God's forgiveness mean that we can continually disobey Him without consequence? Certainly not. For every action there is a reaction, and for every sin there is a consequence. But God's love means that we cannot "out-sin" His ability to forgive us.

How much does God love you? To answer that question, you need only to look at the cross. God's love for you is so great that He sent His only begotten Son to die for your sins and to offer you the priceless gift of eternal life. You must decide whether or not to accept God's gift. Will you ignore it or embrace it? Will you return it or neglect it? Will you invite Christ to dwell in the center of your heart, or will you relegate Him to a position of lesser importance? The decision is yours, and so are the consequences. So choose wisely...and choose today.

More from God's Word

Jesus said to her, "I am the resurrection
and the life. The one who believes in me will live,
even though they die; and whoever lives
by believing in me will never die."

JOHN 11:25–26 NIV

I tell you the truth, anyone who believes
has eternal life.

JOHN 6:47 NLT

Sing to the LORD, all the earth;
proclaim his salvation day after day.

1 CHRONICLES 16:23 NIV

And we have seen and testify that the Father
has sent the Son as Savior of the world.

1 JOHN 4:14 NKJV

If we say, "We have no sin," we are deceiving
ourselves, and the truth is not in us. If we confess our
sins, He is faithful and righteous to forgive us our sins
and to cleanse us from all unrighteousness.

1 JOHN 1:8–9 HCSB

More Thoughts about God's Love

For those who have forsaken God's path of sexual fulfillment, and walked into homosexual intercourse or heterosexual extramarital adultery, Jesus offers astonishing mercy.

JOHN PIPER

Can a person who is a homosexual go to heaven? If he has been saved by the grace of God, yes. But the person loses his reward. There is no earthly peace, no joy, no happiness, no matter what the person says.

CHARLES STANLEY

There is no limit to God. There is no limit to His power. There is no limit to His love. There is no limit to His mercy.

BILLY GRAHAM

God is the giver, and we are the receivers. And His richest gifts are bestowed not upon those who do the greatest things, but upon those who accept His abundance and His grace.

HANNAH WHITALL SMITH

There is no pit so deep that God's love is not deeper still.

CORRIE TEN BOOM

30

The Question

The world seems to grow crazier by the day.
During these troubled times, I know that
I need Jesus. What does the Bible
say about following Christ?

The Answer

God's Word makes it clear: we are all called
to follow in Christ's footsteps. So when it comes
to discipleship, you owe it to yourself, to your
family, and to your Creator to be a devoted
follower of the One from Galilee.

*Yes, there's a raging cultural battle, but the Bible
says we don't use the weapons of this world, and
you overcome evil with good; bless those who
curse you. These attackers are not the enemy;
they are the mission field—they are people
that Jesus shed His precious blood for.*

RICK WARREN

Follow Him

*Then He said to them all, "If anyone wants
to come with Me, he must deny himself,
take up his cross daily, and follow Me."*
LUKE 9:23 HCSB

As you move through and beyond your time of grief, you must walk with Jesus every day. Jesus loved you so much that He endured unspeakable humiliation and suffering for you. How will you respond to Christ's sacrifice? Will you take up His cross and follow Him—during good times and hard times—or will you choose another path? When you place your hopes squarely at the foot of the cross, when you place Jesus squarely at the center of your life, you will be transformed.

Elisabeth Elliot had this advice for believers everywhere: "Choose Jesus Christ! Deny yourself, take up the cross, and follow Him, for the world must be shown. The world must see, in us, a discernible, visible, startling difference."

Today, do your part to take up the cross and follow Him, even if your heart is heavy. When you're traveling step-by-step with the Son of God, you're always on the right path.

More from God's Word

*But whoever keeps His word, truly in him the love
of God is perfected. This is how we know we
are in Him: The one who says he remains in Him
should walk just as He walked.*

1 JOHN 2:5–6 HCSB

For we walk by faith, not by sight.

2 CORINTHIANS 5:7 HCSB

*Take my yoke upon you, and learn of me;
for I am meek and lowly in heart: and ye
shall find rest unto your souls. For my yoke is easy,
and my burden is light.*

MATTHEW 11:29–30 KJV

*Walk in a manner worthy of the God
who calls you into His own kingdom and glory.*

1 THESSALONIANS 2:12 NASB

*Whoever is not willing to carry the cross and follow
me is not worthy of me. Those who try to hold on to
their lives will give up true life. Those who give up
their lives for me will hold on to true life.*

MATTHEW 10:38–39 NCV

More Thoughts about Discipleship

A disciple is a follower of Christ.
That means you take on His priorities as your own.
His agenda becomes your agenda.
His mission becomes your mission.
CHARLES STANLEY

Choose Jesus Christ! Deny yourself, take up the cross, and follow Him, for the world must be shown. The world must see, in us, a discernible, visible, startling difference.
ELISABETH ELLIOT

Christ lives with every person who puts his trust in Him.
BILLY GRAHAM

The crucial question for each of us is this: what do you think of Jesus, and do you yet have a personal acquaintance with Him?
HANNAH WHITALL SMITH

Be assured, if you walk with Him and look to Him and expect help from Him, He will never fail you.
GEORGE MÜLLER